Contents

D0521956

Communities 4

Firefighters in the community 6

What firefighters do 8

Where firefighters work 10

What firefighters use 12

What firefighters wear 16

How firefighters help us 20

Picture glossary 22

Index 23

Notes for parents and teachers 24

Communities

People live in communities. They live near each other and help each other.

People work together in a
community.

Firefighters in the community

Firefighters work in communities.

Firefighters help keep people safe.

What firefighters do

Firefighters help put out fires.

Firefighters help people escape
from fires.

Where firefighters work

Firefighters work at fire stations.

Some firefighters sleep at the fire stations.

What firefighters use

Firefighters use fire engines.

ladder

Fire engines have ladders.

hose

Fire engines have hoses. The water in the hose puts out fires.

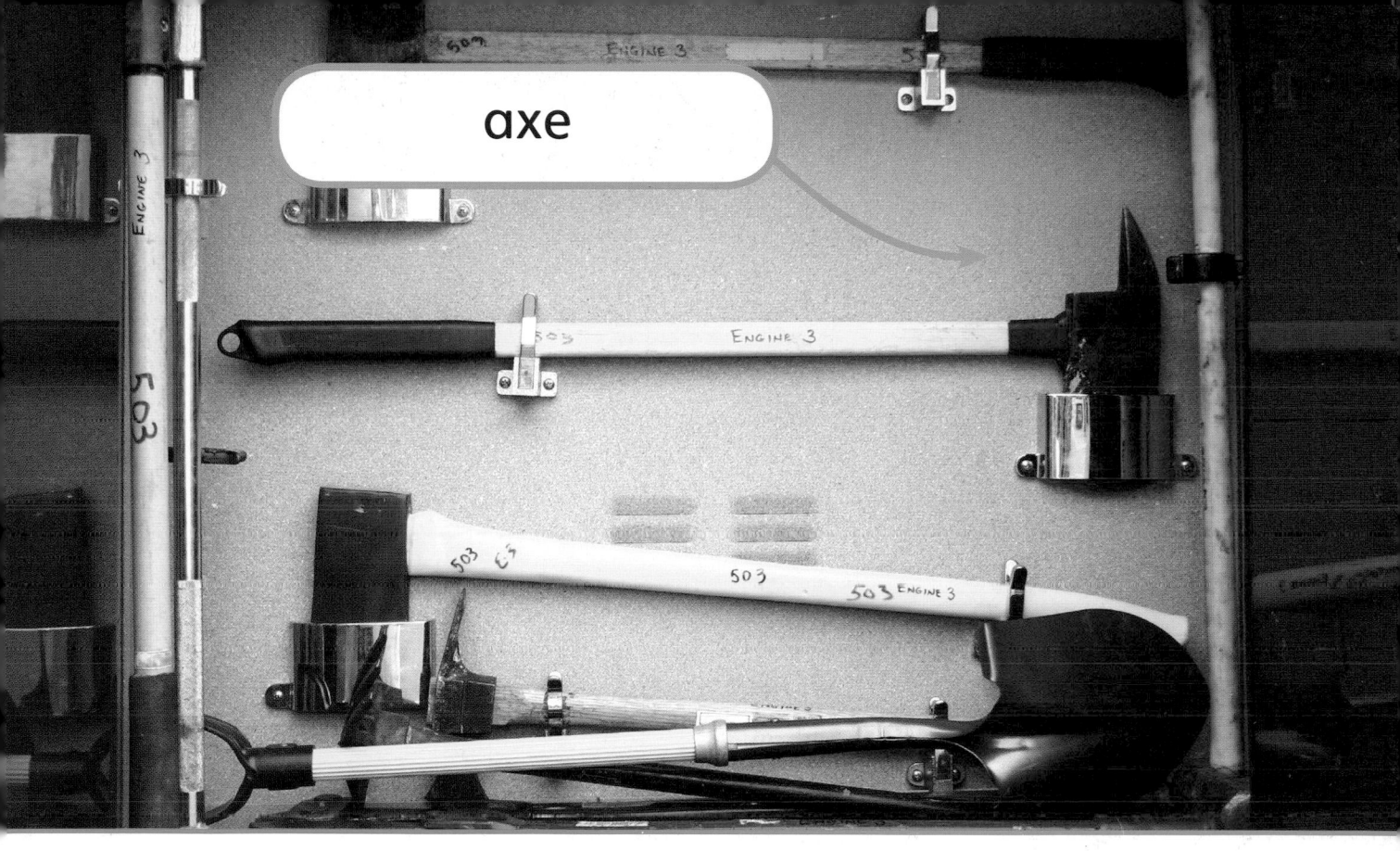

axe

There are lots of different tools in a fire engine.

What firefighters wear

Firefighters wear special jackets.

Firefighters wear special helmets.

Firefighters wear thick gloves.

Firefighters wear big boots.

How firefighters help us

Firefighters help us to stay safe.

Firefighters help the community.

Picture glossary

community group of people living and working in the same area

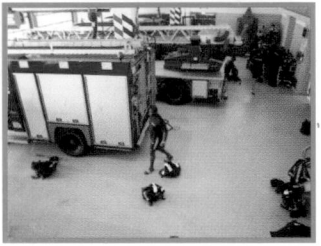

fire station place where fire engines are kept. Firefighters work and sleep at fire stations.

Index

boots 19

communities 4, 5, 6, 21

fire engines 12, 13, 14, 15

fires 8, 9

fire stations 10, 11

gloves 18

helmets 17

jackets 16

staying safe 7, 20

Notes for parents and teachers

This series introduces readers to the lives of different community workers, and explains some of the different jobs they perform around the world. Some of the locations featured in this book include Atlanta, USA (page 4); Colwyn Bay, Wales (page 14); Nuremberg, Germany (page 16); Beijing, China (page 17); Los Angeles, USA (page 18), and New York, USA (page 20).

Before reading
Talk to the children about what a community is. Talk about people who help others in a community. Ask the children what firefighters do. Do they have a fire engine toy at home? What does it look like? Have they ever seen firefighters in action?

After reading
• To the tune of Frere Jacques sing: *Firefighter, firefighter; You are so brave, you are so brave; Putting out the fires, Helping all the people; Saving lives, saving lives.*
• Make junk-model fire engines. Show the children pictures of fire engines. Ask them to think of the features they need to include. What will they use to make the hose and the ladders? Encourage the children to play with the fire engines and put out a fire, or rescue a person.